Buying a Franchise

Tips, Tools & Tales for Doing It Right

BY CAROLYN HERFURTH AND BEV BACHEL

Published by
Idea Girls
722 7th Street SE
Minneapolis, MN 55414

Design and layout
GooseInk
3129 Elliot Avenue South
Minneapolis, MN 55407

ISBN-10: 0-9791833-0-8
ISBN-13: 978-0-9791833-0-0

Printed in the United States of America
First printing

"This book breaks down the fears that stop people from taking action and outlines the steps needed to set and achieve goals. It mixes interesting facts with inspirational quotes and personal stories. In less than two hours, you'll learn all the basics—and find plenty to return to when you need a little motivation."

—Stacy Freeborg, Editor,
Franchise Times

"*Buying a Franchise* isn't just a great primer on the world of franchising— it's an informative guide to business ownership in general."

—Michael Myhre, State Director,
Minnesota Small Business Development Centers

"This is a 'must read' for anyone considering buying a franchise. The tools to help you clarify your goals and objectives are essential to beginning your search and the tips for overcoming obstacles will ensure you don't get sidetracked."

—Ernie Valeski, Director of Franchise Development,
Fantastic Sams of Minnesota

"Talk about cutting to the chase: Carolyn Herfurth and Bev Bachel kick it into warp drive in *Buying a Franchise*. Concise, concrete and amazingly complete."

–Dick Schaaf, Author,
Keeping the Edge: Giving Customers the Service They Demand

Many thanks to the Purple team for your ongoing coaching and inspiration. And to Michael for your total honesty and unwavering support.

—Carolyn

To Steve, for all the reasons you know (and some you don't).

—Bev

Foreword

As a franchise consultant who has helped hundreds of people buy franchises over the past five years, I've learned that it's easy to *buy* a franchise, but not so easy to *choose* the right one.

I hear stories every day from franchisees who rushed through the buying process. These business owners made the fatal mistake of relying on emotions instead of cold, hard facts. As a result, their imagined ticket to paradise became the fast track to unhappiness and, in some cases, financial difficulties.

When done right, purchasing a franchise can be an excellent decision. That's why I recommend *Buying a Franchise*. It lays the foundation for defining your goals and beginning your search. It's also the perfect steppingstone to working with a professionally trained franchise consultant, someone who can save you time and money—as well as a few headaches.

Whatever franchise you might buy in the future, I commend your decision to read *Buying a Franchise* today. Keep it by your side as a helpful reminder of what it takes to buy a franchise. Follow the advice in it, and you'll be well on your way to owning a successful franchise.

—Bruce Krebs, Franchise Consultant, The Entrepreneur's Source

CONTENTS

Introduction

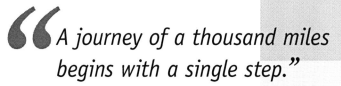

A journey of a thousand miles begins with a single step."

—Chinese proverb

Buying a franchise can feel overwhelming. But it doesn't have to be. That's why we've written this book. It's based on our personal experience helping hundreds of franchise buyers and other business owners select, buy and run successful businesses ranging from advertising to coffee shops to lawn care services.

In the process, we've noticed that people who have clear goals enjoy greater happiness and success than people who don't. But having goals is just the first step. Whether you're eyeing an established franchise or hoping to jump on a hot new trend, your goals are only as good as the steps you take to achieve them.

To point your steps in the right direction, we've assembled dozens of our favorite tips, tools and tales into one book. Our advice will help you better understand the world of franchising and how to choose the franchise that's right for you.

By picking up this book, you've already taken one positive step on your franchise journey. Consider us your friendly guides as you continue along the way!

—Carolyn Herfurth and Bev Bachel

Franchise Basics

What is franchising?

FRANCHISING IS A WAY of distributing goods and services.

When one party pays another for the privilege of selling goods or services...

using a brand, trademark or advertising...

and the parties share an ongoing interest in the business' success...

and one party provides the other with a system for how to run the business...

you have a franchise.

Zors and zees

 **IN THE FRANCHISE WORLD,** you need to know your zors from your zees.

ZORS. Franchisors are businesses that license their trade name (brand) and operating systems (methods for doing business) to franchisees. Zors usually are successful business owners who franchise their concept to expand their market reach and grow without having to add significant staff or spend all their own money.

ZEES. Franchisees are individuals who agree to buy a franchise and operate it according to the terms of a franchise agreement. Zees pay zors for the right to do business under a specific trade name and use the franchisor's operating systems. In exchange, zees typically receive initial training and ongoing support.

Curves ■ Batteries Plus ■ Cinnabon ■ BC Roosters ■ McDonald's ■ Money Mailer ■ The Little Gym ■ Spring-Green Lawn Care ■ Subway ■ Liberty Fitness ■ The Entrepreneur's Source ■ ComputerTots/Computer Explorers ■ The Maids ■ 1-800-DRY-CLEAN ■ Express Personnel ■ Cartridge World ■ AirEnalysis ■ Handyman Matters ■ CLIX ■ Educational Outfitters ■ FastSigns ■ Huntington Learning Centers ■ Senior Helpers ■ Microtel ■ Vendstar ■ Medical Billing ■ Monthly Coupons ■ eAuction Depot

The franchise way

WHEN KEN BOYD'S HIGH-TECH employer reorganized, he found himself without a job. Prospects within his industry and the general job market were few and far between. What's more, Ken wasn't even sure he wanted to continue working in corporate America.

However, Ken did know one thing: He was a great marketer who derived satisfaction from developing and implementing marketing plans that deliver results. Ken realized that the key to his personal fulfillment was to build a business that used his talents. With this knowledge in hand, Ken set out to seek his fortune as a business owner.

Initially, Ken considered starting his own marketing consulting firm, but after researching the idea, he realized how hard it would be to start a business from scratch. That's when Ken began thinking about owning a franchise.

After investigating several, Ken landed on Business Partner, a one-stop marketing shop that offers a range of services, including graphic and Web site design, printing, video production and more. Now, he's marketing his own business—and helping others market theirs.

How big is franchising?

Don't believe us?

TAKE A LOOK AT these numbers for U.S. franchises:

- In 2001, there were more than **767,000** franchised businesses.

- In the same year, franchises created **one out of every seven jobs** and employed more than **8 million** people.

- It is estimated that there are more than **5,000** franchises operating in more than **75 different industries**.

- About **500** new franchise concepts were introduced in 2005 alone.

- Approximately **one out of every 12** businesses is a franchised business.

- A new franchised business opens **every eight minutes!**

Options, options, options!

BUSINESS MODELS VARY WIDELY. There are the obvious differences such as the product or service being sold. Other differences include:

Customers. Some franchises sell to other businesses (B2B), some sell to consumers (B2C) and some sell to both businesses and consumers. For instance, Shred-it typically sells to businesses, Planet Beach to consumers and The UPS Store to both businesses and consumers.

Employees. Some franchises require no, or just a few, employees, while others are labor intensive. Employees range from teenagers to moms to retirees, from blue-collar laborers to trained technicians to college-degreed professionals. Their hours vary widely as well—from seasonal to part-time to full-time to on-call.

Hours. Some franchises are open around the clock, some not at all. Some require full-time attention, while others allow part-time, passive, semi-absentee or even absentee ownership.

Think outside the brick

ALTHOUGH MANY FRANCHISES ARE traditional brick-and-mortar businesses, you may want to consider businesses that are:

- Home-based
- Mobile
- Online
- Virtual

Facing franchise fees

Initial investment

Initial franchise fee   The initial fee you pay to have the right to operate a
                          franchise; 80% of the time, this fee is $25,000-$40,000

Start-up costs   Your expenses for such things as a lease, site build-out,
                          furniture, fixtures, equipment and inventory

Working capital   The money you'll need to operate the business until it's
                          able to support itself (aka cash flow)

Ongoing investment

Royalty payments   The amount you pay a franchisor to use its business
                          model, name and products; typically 5-10% of
                          your revenue

Advertising fees   A fee you pay your franchisor for national advertising
                          efforts, usually 1-3% of your revenue

**TIP: When determining how much you can afford to pay for a franchise, don't forget
to consider your living expenses. How much is your mortgage? How much do you
need for utilities, groceries, gas and other daily living expenses? What about for
insurance, taxes and other expenses?**

Money makes the franchise world go 'round

ALTHOUGH THE AMOUNT OF money required to buy a franchise varies, you'll need at least $20,000 in liquid assets (cash, securities and home equity) and a net worth of $100,000 or more to meet the investment requirements of most franchisors.

For example, the initial investment for a Sytem4 cleaning franchise is less than $20,000 and includes initial equipment and training—and even guaranteed customers.

Some franchisors require much more. Yum! Brands—which includes A&W, KFC, Long John Silver's, Pizza Hut and Taco Bell—requires a minimum of $360,000 in liquid assets and a net worth of $1 million. Yum! also requires that your management team have at least three years of operations experience.

TIP: Ask the franchisors you're considering if they provide financial assistance. A 2006 report from the International Franchise Association Educational Foundation and FRANdata, a franchise information resource center, estimates that 20% of franchisors are willing to help franchisees get started by offering direct financial assistance.

Dollars and cents

FRANCHISE COSTS VARY CONSIDERABLY from one to the next. Here are some examples.

Closet Tailors
Shop-at-home semi-custom closet, garage, pantry and laundry room systems
Initial franchise fee: $14,950   *Initial investment:* $49,950 + truck

Freedom Boat Club
Gives boat lovers the luxury of owning a boat—without having to clean, maintain or house it
Initial franchise fee: $25,000   *Initial investment:* $176,300-$539,400

It's a Grind Coffeehouse
A blues-inspired coffee shop
Initial franchise fee: $36,000   *Initial investment:* $241,500-$440,000

Proforma
Business products such as business documents, commercial printing, promotional and office supplies
Initial franchise fee: $39,500   *Initial investment:* $52,000-$60,000

TIP: Don't assume the most expensive franchise will deliver the best earnings.

Q&A

WON'T IT BE CHEAPER TO START MY OWN BUSINESS THAN TO PAY A FRANCHISE FEE?

Get out your calculator. To start a business from scratch, how much time will you need to figure out what that business will be and how it will operate? How much will you pay to trademark a business name and hire a graphic designer to develop your logo and promotional materials? How much will your point-of-sale system cost? Your initial inventory? Your training? These are just a few expenses you face when starting a business from scratch.

WON'T ROYALTY PAYMENTS BE EXPENSIVE?

Consider royalty payments an investment in your future success. Most franchisors use royalties to create new products and services, develop cross-selling opportunities and fund technology.

HOW CAN I BE SURE I'LL SUCCEED?

In franchising, as in life, there are no guarantees. If franchising were a surefire way of becoming rich and successful, everyone would be doing it. However, franchising does minimize the risk of business ownership.

Entry ways

Single-unit franchising. You buy one unit (aka a territory or store). This might be a brick-and-mortar franchise such as Dry Cleaning Station, a mobile franchise such as 1-800-GOT-JUNK or a home- or office-based business such as The Interface Financial Group. Single units are the most common type of franchise.

Multi-unit franchising. After buying one unit, you purchase a second unit (or more) at a later date. Because you can't be in several places at once, you hire a manager to run each unit, and you manage the managers.

Area development. This method is similar to multi-unit franchising. The main difference is that you commit in advance to opening several units within a specified time frame. Some franchisors require the full fee for all the units up front, while others request just a portion up front and an additional amount each time you open a new unit.

Master franchising. Also known as subfranchising, master franchising gives you the right to develop the franchise concept within a specific geographic area. You're responsible for finding, selecting, training and supporting the subfranchisees in your area.

Reasons for Change

The job security myth

WORRIED THAT BUYING A franchise means giving up job security?

We're in a brave new career economy. As companies continue to downsize, employees continue to feel less secure. Those who do keep their jobs often work longer hours for less money and fewer benefits.

Our point? Sometimes job security isn't secure at all.

“*The more you seek security, the less of it you have. But the more you seek opportunity, the more likely it is that you will achieve the security that you desire.*”

Brian Tracy, author

Is franchising right for you?

FRANCHISE OWNERSHIP COULD BE right for you if you have...

Control issues
- Are tired of office politics
- Resent being micromanaged
- Desire to be your own boss

Economic needs
- Have been downsized
- Are not ready to retire
- Have reached the corporate ceiling

Lifestyle issues
- Want flexibility
- Are willing to work hard but want more work/life balance
- Want to use a business as a vehicle to achieve your goals

Wealth-creation goals
- Are tired of poor raises
- Want to achieve your own goals, not someone else's
- Are looking to build equity in a business you can sell

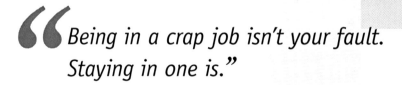

" *Being in a crap job isn't your fault. Staying in one is.*"

Sally Hogshead, author

Who's in charge?

YOU!

SOME POTENTIAL FRANCHISEES FEAR they'll have no creative freedom or control over their business. This concern, while understandable, is unfounded.

The franchisor's responsibility is to establish the business systems. You, the franchisee, are in charge of managing, marketing and promoting the business—all areas in which you can exercise a great deal of creativity.

In fact, many franchise product and service innovations are the result of franchisee suggestions. For example, McDonald's started out with a no-frills selection of hamburgers, shakes and fries. Today, you can find numerous choices on the menu, including ones Ray Kroc never even imagined when establishing his franchise system.

Where did all those great ideas come from? You guessed it…many of them, including the Big Mac, came from franchisees.

Land of the free?

ARE YOU LOOKING FOR more freedom in your career? Business ownership has many pluses, but don't assume that unfettered living is one of them.

When you're an employee, you do your job, report to your manager and collect your paycheck. It's not so simple when you're the one in charge.

Owning a business takes drive and commitment. You'll likely have to manage employees, customers, vendors, a landlord, a lawyer, an accountant and even the IRS.

But, if you buy a good business and are good at what you do, you can earn more money and enjoy more free time than most people. For example, in exchange for months filled with 60-hour weeks, Bev just spent four weeks on a beach in Panama (and called her office only once).

Wanted: team players

IF YOU THINK BUYING a franchise will bring you independence by letting you be your own boss, you're right.

And you're wrong.

It's true that you'll get to call the shots, write your own schedule and make your own business decisions. These are among the great benefits of owning a franchise. But don't forget that you'll also have to sign a contract requiring you to abide by the franchisor's rules.

Think of the franchisor as your coach and yourself as the quarterback. The coach gives you the playbook. But remember, you have the ability to decide which plays to run.

That's why being a team player is so essential. Make sure you trust and respect the franchise leaders you'll be working with and understand how involved they'll be in the day-to-day activities of the business.

Assess Yourself

Are you a goal getter?

ONLY 3% OF ADULTS have clear, written goals. That means 97% of us aren't realizing our full potential.

What a shame, especially since those with clear goals and step-by-step action plans for achieving them accomplish 10 times more than others. In fact, a person who sets goals—and focuses on taking small steps to achieve them—will run circles around a genius who talks a lot but never does anything.

Use goals to bring yourself closer to your dream of owning a franchise.

Write your goals down. Post them on your computer monitor. Carry them in your wallet. Do whatever it takes to keep your goals in sight.

TIP: Having concrete goals increases your confidence and helps you feel more in control. What's more, people who regularly keep a journal or other written record pertaining to their aspirations are 32% more likely to feel they are making progress in their lives.

Why goals are worth having

1. **GOALS HELP YOU BE WHO YOU WANT TO BE.** You can have all the dreams in the world, but if you don't act on them, how will you get where you want to go? When you set goals, you create a path that takes you toward the future you want.

2. **GOALS BOOST YOUR CONFIDENCE.** When you achieve your goals, you prove to yourself and others that you've got what it takes to get things done.

3. **GOALS GIVE YOUR LIFE PURPOSE.** When you're going after your goals, you're less likely to feel bored or waste time.

4. **GOALS HELP YOU TURN THE IMPOSSIBLE INTO THE POSSIBLE.** Goals break down seemingly out-of-reach dreams into small, manageable steps, turning your "someday" hopes into real-life accomplishments!

Get SMART

WHEN WRITING GOALS, MAKE THEM SMART.

Savvy goals are easy to understand, ignite your passion and are meaningful to you.

Measurable goals define the exact outcome you want to achieve.

Active goals use "do it" verbs that keep you moving forward.

Reachable goals are realistic based on your own skills and experience.

Timed goals have specific deadlines by when you'll be able to say, "I did it!"

Not-so-savvy goal
Help others.

Savvy goal
Own a fitness club.

Not-so-measurable goal
Make money.

Measurable goal
Earn $100,000 a year.

Not-so-active goal
Learn about franchising.

Active goal
Meet with three fitness franchises.

Not-so-reachable goal
Become the world's
largest franchisee.

Reachable goal
Buy my first franchise.

Not-so-timed goal
Start my business.

Timed goal
Hold my grand opening by June 15.

Outside-in vs. inside-out

MANY PEOPLE LOOK FOR a franchise from the outside-in. They chat with friends, surf the Web and browse magazines, all while looking for a business that sounds fun, interesting or easy. But just because going out to eat is fun doesn't mean owning a restaurant would be.

Take an inside-out approach instead. In addition to setting **SMART** goals, ask yourself:

- What are my likes and dislikes?
- What are my strengths and weaknesses?
- What needs must my business accommodate?
- How much can I comfortably afford to invest?
- How much do I need to earn? Want to earn?

Also consider various characteristics of your ideal business:

Employees. How many? What type? Teens, professionals, manual laborers, skilled technicians? Part-time? Full-time? Subcontractors?

Hours. Do you want to work Monday through Friday, weekends, business hours, retail hours? Or do you prefer a flexible schedule?

Location. Do you want to work from home, at a store or in an office? What about owning a mobile business?

Sales. Are you willing to proactively prospect and network for business, or do you prefer sales come to you?

Customers. Do you want to sell to businesses, consumers or both?

Financial. What can you afford to invest? How much do you want to make today? In three years? In 15?

Size. Are you interested in a single unit or a larger territory? Or do you have even bigger plans?

What's your style?

ARE YOU AN:

A. Introvert
B. Extrovert
C. Somewhere in between

Whether you're an introvert, extrovert or intro-extrovert, you can find a franchise model that matches your style.

For instance, businesses located in busy shopping malls may be better choices for introverts because customers are likely to come to you. On the other hand, extroverts may prefer business-to-business ventures. Rather than waiting for customers to walk in the door, you go out and find your customers by calling them on the phone or visiting them in their homes or offices.

As you explore franchises, be sure to evaluate what each will require of you. Do you have the personality to ensure the business you're considering succeeds? Or is another business model a better fit?

Can you afford it?

WHEN CONSIDERING YOU AS a franchisee, franchisors look closely at your financial situation. They'll want to make sure you have enough money for the initial investment and that you qualify for additional start-up capital.

The two numbers they look at most closely are:

1. Net worth—the difference between what you own and what you owe
2. Liquidity—how much cash you have available to invest

Use the next two pages to help you determine a comfortable investment range.

Calculate your net worth

Assets—What you own

Cash in checking and savings	$ _____
Value of real estate	$ _____
Stocks/bonds/securities	$ _____
Retirement plan/IRA/401(k) plan	$ _____
Equity in business owned	$ _____
Cash value of life insurance	$ _____
Market value of autos	$ _____
Value of personal possessions	$ _____
Money owed to you	$ _____
Other assets	$ _____
Total Assets	$ _____

Liabilities—What you owe

Notes payable $ _____

Mortgage principal $ _____

Auto loans $ _____

Credit cards $ _____

Charge accounts $ _____

Taxes payable $ _____

Other liabilities $ _____

Total Liabilities $ _____

Total Assets $ _____

(–) Total Liabilities $ _____

YOUR TOTAL NET WORTH: $_____

Funding your franchise

ACCORDING TO A RECENT STUDY by the Small Business Administration (SBA), 66% of start-ups are funded with personal money. Surprisingly, business bank loans only contribute 12% of start-up costs. Here's how most business owners get their funding:

1. **Personal assets.** Includes savings, investments and second mortgages. Some people even tap into their retirement accounts.
2. **Friends and family.** If you borrow from those you know, write a letter of agreement and hire an attorney to review it.
3. **Credit cards.** 9% of business owners use plastic to get started.
4. **Banks.** If you plan to apply for a loan, start building a relationship with a banker today.
5. **Franchisors.** More than 50% of franchisors help franchisees obtain financing. Some offer direct financial assistance; others have relationships with outside lenders and lessors.

Consider an SBA loan

FLIPPING OVER THE MATTRESS and raiding the piggy bank aren't the only ways to finance a franchise.

Although you'll need to bring some capital to the table, you can supplement your cash with a Small Business Administration (SBA) loan.

Twenty percent of franchisors participate in the Franchise Registry Program. Through this program, you benefit from a streamlined process when applying for an SBA-guaranteed loan through private lenders.

SBA loans require less equity than traditional loans and perhaps even minimal collateral. Borrowers can also benefit from an extended amortization schedule, which can lower payments substantially.

For more information, visit www.sba.gov.

TIP: Although each individual situation varies, you'll typically need one-third of your total investment in cash before receiving an SBA loan. For instance, if your total investment is $100,000, you'll need about $33,000 in cash to secure an SBA loan of $67,000.

Rolling over...

...a retirement fund.

ANNE LINDQUIST THOUGHT BUSINESS ownership was out of reach because so many of her assets were in her retirement account. But the light bulb went on for Anne when she learned she could use the money in her 401(k) penalty-free to fund a business.

Thanks to this entrepreneur-friendly finance program, Anne now owns her own business: Inches-A-Weigh, an upscale nutrition and on-site exercise center for women over 40.

She's generating a good income and building equity she can tap into when she and her husband retire. What's more, she owns a business her four 20-something children can participate in if they choose.

TIP: Several companies—including SD Cooper, Guidant Financial and Benetrends—specialize in facilitating penalty-free withdrawals from your 401(k) or IRA.

Emotional capital

AS YOU CONSIDER BUYING a franchise, you'll likely hear many warnings against taking the plunge if you're undercapitalized. These warnings typically refer to money. But don't overlook the importance of emotional capital.

Emotional capital is the encouragement you need to take risks, the support you need to get through tough times and the praise you need to feel good about your accomplishments.

Robin Toboz understands the value of emotional capital. When her husband Rick was considering buying a franchise, she worried the business wouldn't provide enough money to pay for their two sons' college educations. Rick took Robin's concern seriously and addressed it.

A year after Rick bought his franchise, Robin exclaimed, "Rick should have done this five years ago. Even his worst day as a franchise owner is better than his best day in corporate America."

A family affair

IF YOU HAVE A FAMILY, buying a franchise means adjustments for all. New work hours, priorities and finances affect everyone in your household. Before making your decision, involve each family member.

- Think about how your new business will affect your family, especially in the beginning. How do you plan to balance family priorities with the demands of your new business?

- Generate support for your new adventure. Get your family excited about what you're doing and where it'll take you—all of you.

- Make sure everyone knows what to expect as you get the business up and running and how long it might take.

TIP: If you decide to involve family members directly in your business, create defined roles and responsibilities for everyone. Discuss personal space issues as well—working and living together can be challenging!

Partner up

IF YOU'RE CONSIDERING A PARTNER, be sure to choose wisely.

• Do your goals and business philosophies align?

• Are you equally dedicated to the venture?

• Are you both financially secure?

• How will your work styles blend?

Make sure you know the answers to these questions before making a commitment.

TIP: Good contracts make good partners, so create a partnership agreement with the help of an attorney early on.

Are you willing?

BEFORE BUYING A FRANCHISE, ask yourself two questions:

1. **Am I willing to follow a proven system to increase my chances of success?**

2. **Am I willing to pay an upfront franchise fee and ongoing royalties to have access to that system?**

If you're not going to follow the system, why pay for it? But if you are willing to take advantage of the franchisor's proven system—and willing to pay for the privilege of doing so—owning a franchise could be right for you.

Top 10 traits of successful franchise buyers

CAROLYN AND HER COLLEAGUES work with thousands of franchise buyers each year. Here's their list of the top 10 traits that make franchise buyers successful:

1. They're open minded.
2. They have clearly defined goals.
3. They explore franchises that help them achieve their goals.
4. They have a good credit score and access to cash to cover start-up fees.
5. They have a balanced view—they look at both positives and negatives.
6. Their families support them.
7. They have a desire to learn.
8. They're determined to see projects through to completion and have good follow-through.
9. They're willing to ask for help.
10. They have the ability to recognize, accept and enjoy success.

TIP: According to a recent *Entrepreneur* survey of franchisors, the top qualities of successful franchisees are people skills, general business skills and a willingness to be coached.

What's your formula for success?

NOW THAT YOU'VE LOOKED inward to define your goals and business criteria, document them here.

_____

+_____

+_____

+_____

+_____

+_____

= **SUCCESS**

As you search for the franchise that's right for you, narrow your focus to those that best match your formula for success.

TIP: Recognize that you will probably fine-tune your criteria as you learn more about yourself during your discovery process.

Explore Your Options

Google— informative or overwhelming?

YOU'RE READY TO START investigating franchises. You type the word "franchise" into Google, hopeful that you'll quickly get a list of five to 10 franchises that deserve further attention.

Your search returns more than 100 million hits.

Overwhelming, isn't it?

Let's face it—there are thousands of franchises to choose from. To find one that's right for you, keep your success formula close at hand, and don't rely solely on the Internet.

Avoid information overload

DEBRA WOODARD, A FEISTY 20-year veteran of the insurance industry, decided to escape corporate America and investigate opportunities in franchising.

She was quickly overwhelmed by the volume of information she found. The more she learned, the more questions she had.

With Carolyn's help, Debra was able to get her questions answered and crystallize her goals, making it much easier to focus her search.

Eventually, Debra chose Kitchen Tune-Up, a kitchen and bath improvement franchise she claims she'd never have considered if she'd confined her search to the Internet.

Debra's advice: "Use the Internet to support your franchise investigation, but don't rely on it to choose which franchises to explore."

Hire a franchise consultant

TARGETING THE RIGHT FRANCHISE model is difficult to do on your own. A knowledgeable franchise consultant can focus your search, saving you time, money and headaches.

There are two main types of franchise consultants: brokers and coaches. One main difference between the two is who they represent. A broker represents the franchisor, while a coach works on behalf of you, the buyer.

While both make recommendations, brokers typically don't play an active role during your search. A coach, on the other hand, will help you better understand yourself and your goals to determine which franchise is right for you and actively engage with you throughout your entire franchise search.

TIP: Whether you choose to work with a broker or a coach, find someone you believe will look out for your best interests—not just theirs.

Imagine eating soup with half a spoon. You can do it, but it's likely to take longer and be a whole lot messier.

Hire a franchise consultant, and fill up on success.

In search of a "hot" franchise

SUBWAY HAS BEEN ONE of the world's hottest franchises for the past 15 years. According to the company's director of development, Subway received 148,000 franchise inquiries in 2003.

Yet, only 4,363 franchises were awarded—and only 1,200 of these went to new franchisees. That's less than 1% of the inquiries.

Clearly, getting in on what's "hot" isn't easy. What's more, just because a franchise is hot today doesn't mean it will be tomorrow. Nor does it mean it's the right franchise for you.

WHEN LOOKING FOR A franchise that won't cool off, consider:

Staying power. Businesses that offer products or services that customers always need are better bets than "trendy" enterprises. What can't people do without? Dry cleaning, office supplies, auto repair, haircuts, _____ and _____.

Demographic trends. Aging baby boomers make up a huge segment of today's population. What businesses serve these people? Assisted living, meal-prep services, travel agencies, house cleaning services, _____ and _____.

Societal trends. People are concerned about their health, their financial security and their ability to help their kids achieve their potential. How can you capitalize on these trends? Weight-loss centers, tax-planning services, tutoring, _____ and _____.

Reading the crystal ball

CURRENT FRANCHISE TRENDS CATER to a healthier lifestyle, the aging population, active baby boomers, doting parents and animal lovers, among other things. The fastest-growing segments in recent years include:

- Do-it-yourself meal preparation
- eBay consignment stores
- Pet-related supplies and services
- Fitness centers
- Decorating and home improvement services
- Kids' specialty services and activities
- Cleaning services
- Adult in-home care

These trends alone have spawned hundreds of franchise concepts. Which will be successful in the future? It's tough to know. That's why it's so important to thoroughly investigate your options.

In with the new...

ESTABLISHED FRANCHISES MAY HAVE better name recognition and more robust training and support. But an emerging franchise may offer an exciting, cutting-edge concept or an innovative way of meeting marketplace needs. Weigh the risks and rewards of each.

Doug Imholte, area developer for Wireless Toyz, did just that before choosing his franchise. "I thought about buying into a big-name franchise, but the benefits of opening a start-up franchise outweighed the potential risks for me," he said. "I wanted something I could have a bigger hand in creating."

For others, buying a tested concept is more important. "We weren't ready to take a big risk on a new concept," says Diane Hawe, who owns a mailing services store in Los Angeles with her husband. "We wanted a proven concept, especially because we were first-time business owners."

On the cutting edge

KATE TENNESSEN FELT STUCK. With multiple graduate degrees, Kate knew how to tackle big challenges, yet she was underutilized in her role at a large medical technology company. Each passing day left her feeling more frustrated, worried and, worst of all, fatigued by constant stress.

Kate knew getting a similar high-paying job at a different company was only a change of scenery, not a solution. She needed more: an opportunity to get involved in her community and lead a happier, less stressful life.

After investigating her options, Kate purchased a Supper Thyme USA franchise, a fast-growing meal-prep business with a family-friendly menu and a warm, relaxing environment.

Although educating the community about the convenience of the meal-prep concept is a large part of Kate's role, instead of grinding her teeth from stress and anxiety, Kate's smiling. "I'm having so much fun and am incredibly happy," she enthuses.

David or Goliath?

ACCORDING TO STATISTICS, ONLY 4.5% of franchise systems reach 1,000 units. In fact, the median size of franchise systems is only 80 units—small enough for franchise owners to be on a first-name basis with one another, but hardly enough to build brand awareness.

When assessing the importance of size, consider:

- **Financials.** Is the franchisor earning the majority of its revenue from initial franchise fees or from royalties and/or product sales? If it looks like its franchise fee revenues outweigh its royalty revenue stream, find out why.

- **Brand awareness.** Smaller franchisors may not be able to afford national advertising to create name recognition. How might this impact your business?

- **Culture.** How do you think you'll fit into the franchisor's culture? Do you want to be a big fish in a small pond? Or would you prefer to be part of a larger organization?

What's love got to do with it?

WHEN SEARCHING FOR A franchise, you'll meet many eligible businesses. Each one might make your heart flutter, but will you be happy once the thrill is gone?

Many people make an emotional connection with a franchise right off the bat. Then, they invest months of hard work, only to find out later that it doesn't really meet their needs.

As you shop for franchises, revisit your success formula. Focus on franchises that fit your requirements, and let go of those that don't, even if they tug at your heartstrings.

Practice makes passion

A BIG MYTH AMONG people considering self-employment is that work should be based on a passion. Do what you love and the money will follow, right?

Not always. Blindly relying on passion has spelled disaster for countless entrepreneurs and partially explains why an estimated one-third of new U.S. small businesses fail within two years.

To sidestep the passion trap, get clear on your goals and lifestyle objectives, and only consider franchises that support them.

Denise Shaw took this advice to heart, with great results. "I was interested in buying a children's education franchise because I love helping others," says Denise. "But after a closer look, I realized I'd be tutoring other people's kids, rather than enjoying time with my own son."

Instead, Denise bought a Gotcha Covered Blinds franchise. She still helps people but has more control over her schedule so she's home when her son gets off the school bus.

TIP: Your business will become a passion if it aligns with your goals and helps you live your dreams.

Pick three

Did you enroll in the first college you visited? Probably not.

Did you marry the first person you kissed? Doubtful.

Did you buy the first house you looked at? Unlikely.

Even if you think you know what franchise you want to buy, compare it to at least two others. Does your scalp tingle with excitement at the thought of owning a salon? Explore two other businesses that have nothing to do with hair. Perhaps a sporting goods consignment shop or nutrition-supplement business.

Also investigate entirely different business models—compare a retail pet store to a mobile pet grooming service and a doggie daycare. Or a home-based direct mail business to a mall-based cookie company.

Why consider different options? Because learning about other businesses helps you ask better questions about the one you *think* you want. And asking good questions helps you make good decisions.

Emotional notions

FOR BETTER OR WORSE, emotions play a huge part in any purchase. As you shop for a franchise, keep your emotions in check by staying as objective as possible.

Don't get us wrong—emotions can be great motivators. But they can also diminish your ability to make informed decisions. They can magnify minor problems and blind you to really important issues. Worst of all, they can lead to faulty assumptions based on what you *want* to happen or how you *hope* things will work out.

Take off your rose-colored glasses and set your emotions aside. Instead, pretend you're a detective.

Do your research and get independent verification of your assumptions. Whether you're proven correct, learn something new or discover your logic is flawed, you'll be far better off with facts than emotional notions.

Curb appeal only goes so far

WHEN CAROLYN WAS HOUSE HUNTING, she and her real estate agent pulled up in front of a bright orange house. Carolyn took one look and told the agent to keep driving.

After a heated discussion, her agent convinced her to go inside. And guess what? Carolyn loved the house and has called it home for the past 10 years.

What does this have to do with buying a franchise?

Don't let your first impressions be your only impressions.

You could miss out on the opportunity of a lifetime if you dismiss them without a second glance.

TIP: Even if the business you're considering doesn't have curb appeal, give it a closer look. You just might be surprised at what you find.

Change your point of view.

Open minds open doors

YOU CAN'T JUDGE A book by its cover. Nor can you judge a franchise based on first impressions. Silence your inner critic and open your mind:

- **Get a second opinion.** If you're not sure whether a certain franchise is right for you, ask others what they think.

- **Ask tough questions.** Is your instant dislike of a house-cleaning business really masking a fear of what your neighbors will think? It's fine to have concerns, but be sure you face your real concerns.

- **Remove yourself from the picture.** Instead of focusing on the reasons a business isn't right for you, imagine why it would be perfect for a friend. Now, what's the difference between you and your friend? Personality? Resources? Or maybe…nothing at all.

Half full or half empty?

What you see 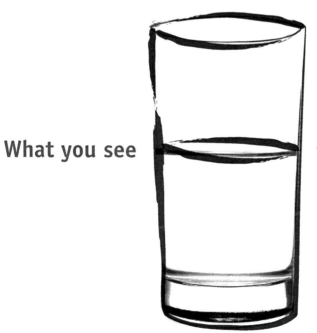 is up to you.

Just the facts, Jack

"The market is saturated."

"There's too much competition."

"Nobody buys _____ anymore."

"My friend knows someone who owned a similar business, and it didn't work."

When you were in school, did your professors let you turn in papers based purely on hypothesis and conjecture, or were you required to substantiate your claims?

Approach your franchise search in the same way you would a term paper. Leave your emotions and opinions at home. Instead, focus your attention on facts. Gather them, analyze them and rely on them.

"*It's not what you don't know that hurts you, it's what you do know that ain't so.*"

Will Rogers, U.S. humorist

Knowledge is power

BEFORE BUYING A FRANCHISE, do your research.

Dive into the Web. Use a search engine such as Google and enter key words and phrases to learn about pricing strategies, competitors, management, marketing and more.

Ask a librarian. Librarians know how to sift through a wealth of resources to find specific information.

Interview experts. Find franchise owners who can tell you about their real-life experiences. Begin with a clear goal of what you'd like to learn, such as, "I'd like to know how you spend your day" or "I'd like a better sense of what to expect in terms of income."

Observe before you buy. A football player watches films of the opposing team before suiting up for a game. You can learn a lot about the new world you're considering by spending time in it.

It pays to be a know-it-all

BUT IT DOESN'T NECESSARILY pay to be a do-it-all.

Many franchise owners don't spend enough time owning up to all the responsibilities of a business owner.

The products or services you sell are just the tip of the iceberg when it comes to the responsibilities of business ownership. Don't get stuck focusing on them during your search.

Remember, in addition to running your business, you'll also be the manager, marketer, negotiator, technology guru and more. That's because your job is to make sure every aspect of your business works to increase your bottom line.

TIP: Read Michael Gerber's *The E-Myth Revisited* to help you determine what to focus on and what you can cost-effectively hire others to do.

Reap the rewards of networking

NETWORKING IS NOTHING MORE than meeting people and building relationships, relationships that grow and have the power to be mutually beneficial. Whether you know it or not, you've probably been reaping the advantages of networking all your life. And you certainly can put it to use now.

TIP: To make the most of networking, spend 75% of your time with people you don't know.

" *Networking works **well** when you employ the two-word secret: **Show up.***

*Networking works **best** when you employ the three-word secret: **Show up prepared.**"*

Jeffrey Gitomer, author

Draft a dream team

ONE GREAT WAY TO get the support you need is by forming your own dream team, a group of key people who believe in you and will help you achieve success. Your dream team can include friends, family, colleagues, neighbors, members of the community and even people you haven't met.

Wait, people you haven't met? How do you draft them? Take a deep breath and pick up the phone or send an e-mail. Bev often contacts interesting people and asks for 15 minutes of their time. She always learns something—and those people sometimes become good friends or important mentors.

Here's how to ask for help:

1. **Introduce yourself.** Be brief and honest. Don't exaggerate. A good opener: "Hi, I'm thinking about buying a franchise and would love to hear what you have to say about your experience."

2. **Compliment the person in a meaningful way.** Explain why you want to meet the person: "I drive past your business every day, and I'm amazed at how full your parking lot always is."

3. **Ask for help.** "Would you be willing to meet with me? I'd like to learn how you promote your business."

TIP: Always say thank you, and remember to return the favor or pay it forward.

20 questions

ALTHOUGH THERE ARE HUNDREDS of questions you can ask, be sure to...

Ask franchisors:

1. What initial and ongoing support is offered? Do I pay extra for this?

2. What national advertising do you do? Who pays for it? What advertising will I need to handle on a local or regional level?

3. How are territories defined? How do you think the franchise will do in my area?

4. Who is your target market? Who are your customers?

5. Who are your competitors? What differentiates you from them?

6. What are the roles and responsibilities of a franchisee?

7. What qualities do successful franchisees exhibit?

8. What would your franchisees say is the biggest challenge of this business?

9. What financial information can you provide in terms of revenue and income?

10. What is the initial investment range of the franchise? How much cash do I need for start-up costs? How much might I expect to borrow?

Ask franchisees:

11. Are you satisfied with your working relationship with the franchisor? Do you feel the franchise organization is fair and easy to work with?

12. What initial and ongoing training and support does the franchisor provide? Are you satisfied with that?

13. How effective are the advertising and marketing programs?

14. What sort of communication and synergies exist among the franchisees?

15. Who is your competition? How do you differentiate yourself?

16. How do you view the long-term viability and future of this franchise?

17. What start-up costs and monthly expenses can I expect?

18. How many and what types of employees do I need?

19. How do you spend your time? What are your responsibilities?

20. How much money can I expect to earn my first year? Second? Third?

TIP: Ask franchisees if they would buy the same franchise again. Their response can speak volumes.

Buy for the bottom line

WE ALL HAVE THE capacity to be successful. The question is: How successful do you want to be, especially when it comes to your own bottom line?

When we asked franchisors to describe characteristics of the franchise owners they consider the most financially successful, they said successful franchise owners:

- **Have clearly defined goals.** It seems obvious, right? Before you go any further in your franchise search, take time to write down your short- and long-term goals. And be sure to refer to them often.

- **Are comfortable talking about money.** When it comes to buying and running a business, it helps to be able to talk about money. Ask others how much they paid and what they make. Be prepared to share the same information.

- **Think big.** Try the "add two zeros" approach to earning more. Decide what you want to earn ($90,000), and then add two zeros ($9,000,000). As the saying goes, shoot for the moon. Even if you miss, you'll land among the stars.

Show me the money

HOW MUCH MONEY WILL you earn if you invest in a franchise and how do you find out?

According to the International Franchise Association, about 25% of franchisors provide some earnings information.

However, don't panic if a franchisor doesn't disclose earnings. You can still get earnings information by speaking with franchisees and asking about average sales revenues, average profit margins and break-even expectations. And you might even walk away with more realistic expectations.

Here's one way to ask franchisees about earnings:

"Based on your personal experience and knowledge of other franchisees, is it reasonable for me to expect to earn $_____ in year one, $_____ in year two and $_____ in year three?"

Invest in a franchise that will invest in you

IS THE FRANCHISE YOU'RE considering committed to training? While most franchisors say they are, the length and quality of their training programs vary.

Only you know how much, or how little, training you need. Advocate for it, and find out what training the franchisor offers:

- Initial?
- Ongoing?
- Hands-on?
- Online?

Also ask franchisees for their take:

- Was the training complete?
- Did it help prepare them for what was to come?
- Did they receive complete documentation?

Culture club or culture shock?

TO GAUGE THE STRENGTH of your potential relationship with a franchisor, you must understand how well you'll fit into the company's culture.

This process begins with the franchise sales representative, who is likely your primary point of contact. His or her style will be an indication of the company's culture, but don't judge the entire franchise system based solely on that individual.

Make an effort to talk with others involved with the franchise. Meet with management. Visit the company's headquarters (many franchisors have a Discovery Day to which they invite potential franchisees) and hang out at the water cooler with the accounts payable clerks or invite the customer service representatives for lunch.

Getting to know these people will give you a better sense of the culture—and help you determine if it's a franchise organization you'll be proud to be associated with.

Does the shoe fit?

VALIDATION IS THE TERM used to describe the process of investigating a franchise. For each franchise you investigate, you'll want to:

1. **Check out the franchisor.** How long has the company been in business? How many franchises has it sold? What are its growth plans? Does it have a well-organized application process and established criteria for awarding franchises?

2. **Visit the franchisor's headquarters.** What support does the franchisor provide? Ask to see proof (e.g., training manuals, ad slicks, Plan-o-grams). Interview employees and talk to executives to get a sense of how they're spending their time. Are they putting out fires or focused on the future?

3. **Interview franchisees.** The best way to learn about the quality of a franchise system is to speak with current franchisees. Call at least three. If possible (and relevant), visit at least one nearby store to see it in action. If you can, ask to shadow the owner for a few hours or several days.

4. **Review financial information.** A franchise must generate enough royalty income to pay all company expenses or the franchisor is vulnerable to problems. Also, note the source of the company's equity. A company's greatest source of revenue shouldn't come from franchise sales income.

5. **Evaluate the name, industry and operating support.** When you buy a franchise, a big part of what you're buying is its reputation. Make certain it's well-regarded. Evaluate the industry. How large is it? Is the product or service a necessity? A luxury? A fad? Also find out about operating support. The franchisor should offer comprehensive support, including training, regular meetings, documentation, product and equipment research and development, software, technical support and more.

UFO-what?

BEFORE YOU BUY A franchise, you'll want to review its Uniform Franchise Offering Circular, commonly referred to as a UFOC.

A UFOC is:

- A document with important information that a franchisor is legally required by the Federal Trade Commission to give you before you buy a franchise.

- Anywhere from several to several hundred pages.

- Generally distributed via hard copy, but many franchisors are now sending it electronically.

- A document that includes information on fees, start-up costs, training, pending litigation, current and former franchisees and the franchisor's audited financial statements.

TIP: Many people choose to have an attorney review all or parts of this disclosure document. Do what's comfortable for you.

Consult the experts

AS YOU NARROW YOUR choices, you're going to have to make a number of decisions, many of which you'll have to live with for a long time. While you don't have to be an expert in every area, you will want to consult the following experts to ensure you're making well-informed decisions:

- **Franchise consultant**—to guide you throughout the process
- **Financial advisor**—to watch over your assets
- **Accountant**—to review your financial projections and business plan
- **Attorney**—to review the license agreement and the Uniform Franchise Offering Circular
- **Commercial real estate agent**—to help you secure a great location

Don't be alarmed if the experts you consult have differing opinions. Getting a variety of opinions will actually strengthen your buying process. And research shows that people increase their productivity when they broaden their point of view.

TIP: Remember, you are asking the experts for their assistance in the area of their expertise. You're not asking them to second-guess your decisions.

For more information, turn to...

American Association of Franchisees & Dealers
PO Box 81887
San Diego, CA 92138-1887
800-733-9858
www.aafd.org

American Franchisee Association
53 West Jackson Blvd., Suite 1157
Chicago, IL 60604
312-431-0545
www.franchisee.org

Association of Small Business Development Centers
8990 Burke Lake Road
Burke, VA 22015
703-764-9850
www.asbdc-us.org

The Council of Better Business Bureaus
4200 Wilson Blvd., Suite 800
Arlington, VA 22203-1838
703-276-0100
www.bbb.org

Federal Trade Commission
600 Pennsylvania Ave. NW
Washington, DC 20580
202-326-2222
www.ftc.gov

International Franchise Association
1501 K Street NW, Suite 350
Washington, DC 20005
202-628-8000
www.franchise.org

SCORE (Senior Corps of Retired Executives)
409 3rd Street SW, 6th Floor
Washington, DC 20024
800-634-0245
www.score.org

Small Business Administration
6302 Fairview Road, Suite 300
Charlotte, NC 28210
800-U-ASK-SBA (800-827-5722)
www.sba.gov

7 ways to save on real estate

IF YOU'LL BE CONDUCTING business from a brick-and-mortar location, land the best deal by using these tips from Paula Anderson, founder of Square Feat, a commercial real estate company:

1. **Engage a tenant representative.** You need someone to look out for your best interests, just like when you buy a home. A tenant representative does this—and represents you with the landlord.

2. **Negotiate your expansion.** Have your representative negotiate the ability for you to expand to the right or left of your space. This gives you the flexibility to expand without the expense of moving.

3. **Negotiate a buyout clause.** This maximizes your flexibility to respond to your growth by giving you a way to get out of your lease so you can move into a larger space, potentially in an entirely different building.

4. **Negotiate the option to renew your lease.** Having the option to renew your lease at market or advertised rates can save you from paying above-market rates when it comes time to renew your lease.

5. **Hire a real estate attorney.** Like a tenant representative, an attorney represents your interests. Be sure the one you hire is knowledgeable about what is acceptable in your market, efficient at reviewing leases and a pro at negotiating with landlords.

6. **Look for "as is" space.** If you're willing to take space as is (saving the landlord from making improvements), you may be able to get better rates or perhaps even free rent for a few months.

7. **Look for sublease options.** If you want a shorter lease, look for subleases; they're often offered at a discount. Talk to a real estate broker or watch the ads in your local paper.

Location, location, location

A FAST-FOOD RESTAURANT likely requires a different location than a daycare center, which may require a different location than an upscale hotel. Your location can decide the fate of your business, so take it seriously.

When determining where to locate your business, consider your customers.

Will they buy on impulse? If so, consider a high-traffic location such as a mall.

Will they be walking or driving? If they're on foot, consider a residential neighborhood. If they're driving, pick a location that's easy to get to.

What other errands might they be doing? If it's likely your customers will be going to the grocery store, pharmacy or post office during the same trip, place your business in their path.

Will they be in a hurry? If your customers want a quick cup of coffee on their way to work or a nutritious dinner on their way home, you'll want a location with easy access—perhaps even one with a drive-thru.

TIP: Most franchisors have criteria for selecting a successful location. Don't disregard their advice.

Overcome Obstacles

What's stopping you?

FEAR—SOMETIMES IT ATTACKS US from all sides. Fear of failure, fear of change, fear of the unknown, fear of abandonment, fear of disappointing others. Even fear of success.

Fear is like a ravenous lion. Instead of feeding on wild prey, fear feeds on ignorance. The franchise search process is your opportunity to collect information and use your newfound knowledge to vanquish your fears.

It's simple: The more you know, the less fearful you'll feel.

Tame your fears by writing them down. Grab a sheet of paper and answer these questions:

1. What are your fears about becoming a franchisee?
2. What are the worst possible outcomes if your fears came true?
3. What do you have to gain if you overcome your fears?

Now, grab a match, set your sheet of paper on fire and watch all your fears go up in smoke.

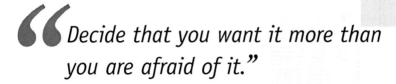

Decide that you want it more than you are afraid of it."

Bill Cosby, comedian

Step out of your comfort zone

WHY DO PEOPLE HAVE a hard time taking the first step toward owning a business? According to Peter McWilliams, author of *Do It! Let's Get Off Our Buts,* it's because there is something we are trained to honor more than our dreams: the comfort zone.

Your comfort zone is the status quo. It's a risk-free place where nothing new happens and where you don't have to take any chances.

Breaking out of your comfort zone can be hard. It takes commitment, action and a conscious decision to make a change. Along the way, it's tempting to quit or get distracted. But when you're 75, how do you want to answer this question:

> **"Throughout my life, did I pursue my dreams,
> or did I do what was comfortable?"**

Don't let your dreams die. Take the first step. We—and hundreds of thousands of other franchise owners—will be waiting for you here in the big world outside your comfort zone!

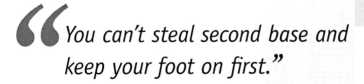

You can't steal second base and keep your foot on first."

Frederick Wilcox, author

No more excuses

MARKET RESEARCH FIRM HARRIS INTERACTIVE asked Americans who were considering starting a business why they hadn't yet done so. Their primary reasons:

- Lack of funding (37%)
- Fear of losing job security (28%)
- No viable business idea or plan (23%)

These responses may seem reasonable, but in reality, they're excuses used to rationalize why these people stay in their comfort zones.

When facing a mountain of potential obstacles, there's one solution: research.

Gathering solid information about your concerns will either validate or invalidate them, leaving you free to get on with your franchise search—and your life.

Woulda, coulda, shoulda

WHEN ASKED TO DESCRIBE significant regrets in their lives, more than eight out of 10 people focused on actions they did not take rather than on actions they did.

In other words, they focused on things they failed to do rather than things they failed at doing.

Ready, set…go!

WHAT'S THE DIFFERENCE BETWEEN a person with good ideas and a successful franchise owner?

Action.

In fact, doing one thing, no matter how small, moves you closer to success. Completing a task—even something as simple as visiting a franchisor's Web site or mentioning your interest in owning a franchise to a friend—triggers the release of endorphins. In other words—you'll feel great!

So what are you waiting for? Get up right now and do one thing that moves you closer to becoming a franchise owner.

Go…

…for green. Talk to a banker.
…for knowledge. Attend a franchise showcase.
…for advice. Call a successful franchise owner and ask her how she got started.

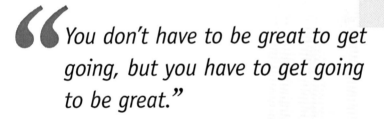

"You don't have to be great to get going, but you have to get going to be great."

Les Brown, author and motivational speaker

It's a matter of time

YOU PROBABLY KNOW PEOPLE who say they're going to buy a cabin, run a marathon or travel to Europe...one day—as soon as they find the time.

If you really want to own a franchise, you have to find the time to make it happen. After all, your most precious asset isn't capital; it's time.
You'll always be busy. There will always be something else that demands your attention. And there will never be a better time.

Obsess about your calendar and to-do list. Examine them each morning, do a post-mortem each night.

Does how you spend your days reflect your priorities?

TIP: Ten minutes of planning at the beginning of your day can actually save you up to 90 minutes once you're working. If you're looking for a way to jumpstart your productivity, begin each day by making a list of what you need to get done. Start with what's most important, not with what's easiest.

Take time to find time

THE AC DOESN'T WORK, your 2-year-old throws a tantrum and your in-laws arrive for a surprise visit—all before you've gotten out of bed!

Wonder how you'll fit in a franchise search? Take a deep breath. Relax. You do have time. Here's how to find it:

Pass on perfection. Does the house need to be spotless? Does dinner need to be homemade? When you focus on "good enough" instead of perfection, you'll be amazed at the extra time you have.

Delegate. Ask friends and family for help with routine responsibilities so you have more time to devote to your franchise search. Teenagers can cook dinner, younger children can fold laundry.

Fill your pockets. Take advantage of downtime while you're commuting to work or waiting in the doctor's office. Listen to a motivational tape, read an article or write a thank-you card.

Kick the procrastination habit

"I need more time to think."

"I'll call my lawyer tomorrow."

"I'm waiting to see what Aunt Prudence (whom I haven't talked to in 20 years) thinks."

Sound familiar? If you truly want to earn your living as a franchise owner, mend your get-to-it-later ways and become a taskmaster!

Confront your BST. All franchise buyers have at least one BST (Big Scary Task) looming. Usually the last to get done, this task is often the most important. Whatever your BST is—doing research, completing your net worth statement, telling your spouse you want to quit your job—do it.

Do it now. Tackle tasks that take five minutes or less while they're fresh in your mind. Putting tasks off has a funny way of making them more daunting later on.

Break down tasks. Breaking tasks into small, bite-size chunks makes big jobs manageable. Instead of saying, "I'm going to call every franchise I'm considering," set a small, concrete goal such as "I will call three franchisors by 5 p.m. today."

Imagine eating an apple in one bite. That's what buying a franchise can feel like unless you break the process into manageable steps.

Calm the critics

YOU KNOW WHO THE NAYSAYERS are in your life: the people who think it's their job to rain on your parade.

Handling criticism is important, especially if the critic is your spouse or significant other. Here's how:

1. **Listen carefully.** Learn as much as possible about their concerns.
2. **Address their concerns.** Use the facts you've uncovered during your franchise investigation.
3. **Repeat: Their intentions are good.** The doubters may not even realize their comments are getting you down. Keep your responses positive and respectful.

Remember, you're the one looking for a business. You're gathering facts and analyzing data so you can feel confident about your decision. Why not use your research to calm the critics in your life, too? Most of them will appreciate hearing the facts, and some might also be impressed with all your hard work!

TIP: If the critics keep talking, smile and say, "Trust me, I've done my homework," and change the subject. And if the critic is the barista at your neighborhood coffee shop or a fifth cousin twice removed, don't even bother. Save your energy for your business!

Take care of your most valuable asset—YOU!

AS YOU RESEARCH FRANCHISES, talk to owners, develop your business plan and move through the purchasing process, remember to take care of yourself. You are vital in the success of your future franchise!

As you dedicate yourself to your new venture, set personal priorities. And stick to them.

Exercise. Eat right. Get adequate sleep. And spend time with your family and friends. Even the CEOs of Fortune 500 companies understand the importance of this: 80% of them say a healthy family life is crucial to a successful business life.

Affirm yourself

AFFIRMATIONS HELP YOU REPLACE negative, self-defeating thoughts with positive ones that "make firm" your dreams of franchise ownership.

If you want to own a franchise, post an affirmation on your bathroom mirror or refrigerator door that says, "I'm the owner of a successful franchise." Then, repeat it often—while in the shower or on the bus, while walking the dog and buying groceries. The more you repeat your affirmations, the more powerful they become.

Here are some to get you started:

"I control my destiny."
"I have flexibility with my schedule."
"I call the shots."
"I can succeed at whatever I put my mind to."
"I have all the money I need."
"Owning this franchise exceeds my expectations."

When writing your affirmations:

Stay in the present. Phrase your affirmations in the present tense, not future tense. For example, affirm, "I am the owner of a wildly successful business," rather than "I will buy a franchise."

Be positive. Affirm what you want, not what you don't want. Say, "I love earning $100,000 a year in my new business," instead of "I don't have to worry about my credit card debt anymore."

Be specific. Like goals, affirmations are most effective when they're specific. For instance, "I'm the proud owner of a Papa Murphy's Pizza store" is better than "I own a business."

Think on your feet

MANAGEMENT CONSULTANT REGINA BARR says quick thinking is a skill every business owner needs. Use these tips to stay on your toes:

Trust. Take this advice from improvisational comedians: If you feel your feet moving—follow them! If you constantly daydream about helping others live healthier lives, consider a fitness or nutrition franchise.

Develop a "yes, and..." mentality. Don't dismiss ideas without giving them a chance. Kick the phrase "yes, but..." to the curb. Instead, get in the habit of using "yes, and..."

> Yes, <u>but</u> where would I get the money?
> Yes, <u>and</u> I will call my banker tomorrow to see if I qualify for a loan.

Take action. Instead of endlessly analyzing your choices, pick the one that seems best and go for it. Taking action increases your focus.

Play. Kids are experts at thinking on their feet. The next time you're with children, watch how quickly they adapt to what's going on.

Dishin' up success

RUTH LUNDQUIST AND DARCY OLSON are co-founders of Let's Dish, a meal-preparation franchise. After building their concept from the ground up, Ruth and Darcy are now expanding nationwide.

Use their advice to get your own franchise cooking:

Listen to your gut. If you have a feeling that something isn't right, explore your feelings. Don't act off-the-cuff from your gut, but use your intuition to help inform your direction and to learn more about things that don't seem quite right.

Be prepared to make quick decisions. You won't always have the perfect amount of research, information and input—and you'll never have all the answers. But you're still going to have to make decisions.

Go for it. You don't want to look back with regret at what could have been. There's power in being able to create your own destiny.

Don't get stuck

NOT FINDING A BUSINESS to buy, especially if you've invested a lot of energy in the process, can leave you feeling disappointed and upset. You may even find yourself replaying what went wrong and what you could have done differently. You may catch yourself repeatedly saying, "If only..." and imagining a better, more positive outcome.

Dwelling on 'if onlys' doesn't get you very far.

Instead, remind yourself of all you learned in the process and congratulate yourself for having the courage and perseverance to try as hard as you did.

You owe it to yourself to keep moving forward.

TIP: Everyone fails or makes mistakes at some point. It's part of being human. In fact, the only sure way of never experiencing failure is by not doing anything. But is that what you really want...to hide from life and avoid any risks?

Will beats skill

YOU DON'T NEED A PH.D. in nutrition to own a fitness business. A Harvard MBA won't make your daycare center an automatic winner. And all the contacts in Martha Stewart's Rolodex can't guarantee your success running a home decor franchise. But there is something that can increase your odds for success.

It's not skill; it's will.

Research shows that will and determination far outweigh other qualities in determining success. Sure, tons of talent and endless education are great. But what you really need is the will to try and the determination to keep going, even when times get tough.

Tune in to the power of positive thinking

MANY BUSINESS OWNERS, EVEN those who seem to have everything going for them, are occasionally plagued by negative thoughts: I'm not good enough. I never succeed in anything. There's no way this is going to work.

Even the two of us sometimes have thoughts like these. They're courtesy of a little voice inside our heads that plays running commentary about everything that's going on.

This voice generally fills your mind with negative thoughts, which is why it's often referred to as your inner critic. But what if this voice was kind and cheery? Wouldn't you feel a lot more confident and positive?

The next time you hear your inner critic complaining, stop listening to it. Instead, tune in to positive thoughts.

Tune out:

"I'm really bad at this."
"I don't know how to make a decision."
"There's no point to this. I'll just fail."
"I can't do anything right."
"I'm too old to try something new."

Tune in:

"I'm great at _____."
"A mistake isn't the end of the world."
"I'm going to give it a try. What's the worst that can happen?"
"I can't expect myself to be perfect. No one is."
"I can do this!"

TIP: Attitude—not talent, money or a college degree—plays a bigger role than you might imagine in determining your success. If you believe you'll succeed, you'll put yourself in a problem-solving frame of mind and more quickly realize your franchise-ownership dreams.

Got a minute?

HERE ARE 10 THINGS you can do—each takes only 60 seconds—to keep your momentum going:

1. Go to www.franchisetimes.com and subscribe to *Franchise Times* magazine and free e-zine.

2. List 10 reasons why you'll succeed as a franchise owner.

3. Ask your spouse to pick up dinner so you can spend time at the library.

4. Visit www.franchisebusinessreview.com to see if there's a free report on any of the franchises you're considering.

5. Subscribe to a daily motivational quote at www.nightingale.com.

6. E-mail colleagues to find out if they can recommend a good accountant or attorney.

7. Revisit your success formula.

8. Call a franchise owner and invite him or her to coffee.

9. Review the information you've collected.

10. Pat yourself on the back—no matter how much more you have to do, take a moment to congratulate yourself for all you've already accomplished.

Go For It

—NOT!

SHOPPING FOR A FRANCHISE can be fun, but your ultimate goal is to buy a franchise—not to spend all your time shopping for one. Research, inquiries, interviews and location scouting are important, but don't get so overwhelmed by your options that you can't make a decision.

Jeff and Trish Johnson were once franchise "shoppers." Despite their best efforts, they weren't able to narrow their choices.

That's when Carolyn came to the rescue. She helped the Johnsons realize they'd done enough shopping. They had all the information they needed to make a decision.

With Carolyn as their guide, Jeff and Trish chose CertiRestore, a furniture restoration business. "We'd still be out shopping if Carolyn hadn't helped us articulate our goals, analyze our options and build our confidence," says Jeff. "Thanks to her proven process, we're now franchise owners, not just franchise shoppers."

There is no perfect 10

CHANCES ARE SLIM THAT you'll ever find a business that's a perfect "10." Rather than drive yourself crazy trying, find one that allows you to answer "yes" to each of these questions:

1. Does this franchise have a solid, well-developed system?

2. Would I enjoy this business?

3. Can I see myself succeeding?

4. Would owning this franchise help me achieve the income and lifestyle goals I've set for myself?

If you can answer "yes" to these questions, you've found a franchise that's right for you.

Sooner or later, you've got to decide

YOU'VE FINALLY NARROWED YOUR search to two or three finalists but aren't sure which franchise to choose. Create a decision matrix.

1. List your goals and other criteria in the first column.

2. Add a column for each franchise that's made it to the "finals."

3. Rank each franchise from 1 (low) to 4 (high) as to how well it meets your goals and criteria.

4. Add up the scores.

5. List any concerns.

What does your decision matrix indicate? Does one column heavily outweigh the others?

Goals / criteria:	Franchise A	Franchise B
Retire in 12 years	4	1
Build equity	4	4
Provide jobs for my kids	4	4
Use my management skills	4	4
Recession resistant	4	3
5-15 employees	4	4
Flexible schedule	3	2
Become semi-absentee in 6-8 years	4	1
No direct sales	3	4
Brick-and-mortar location	4	4
Customers coming to me	4	4
Total initial investment <$200,000	2	3
Initial cash requirement <$75,000	2	2
$100,000 in earnings by year 2	4	1
Total:	**50**	**41**
Concerns:	• I'll have to do some prospecting the first year • Initial cash is $10,000 more than I planned	• Real estate is expensive and difficult to find • High employee turnover

Ready to buy?

YOU'VE DONE YOUR RESEARCH. Contemplated your options. Made your selection. And now you're ready to seal the deal and buy a franchise.

But hold on. You've still got work to do. Even though the finish line is in sight, you still have important decisions to make—and likely could benefit from the expert advice of both an attorney and a CPA. Ask them to review any documents you're planning to sign, including the franchise agreement, the contract that details the terms of your business relationship with the franchisor.

As important as an attorney and CPA are, remember not to let them set the agenda, decide your fate or negotiate on your behalf. Only you should do those things. But you should definitely listen to their advice. Because they have no emotional ties, they're free to speak their minds—and their fresh perspective can prove valuable.

TIP: Hiring experts can be costly. Most lawyers and CPAs bill by the hour—usually hundreds of dollars an hour. Our advice? Ask for a fixed fee ahead of time.

Got it or need it?

Support from your family and spouse   □ **Got it**   □ **Need it**

Capital for start-up costs   □ **Got it**   □ **Need it**

Enough income or savings for your family   □ **Got it**   □ **Need it**
to survive for six to eight months

A business plan, including financial projections   □ **Got it**   □ **Need it**

Leap of faith

ONCE YOU'VE DONE YOUR research, analyzed the data you've collected and chosen a franchise, it's time to take a leap of faith.

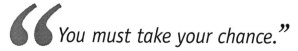 *We must walk consciously only part way toward our goal, and then leap in the dark to our success.*"

—Henry David Thoreau, author

You must take your chance."

—William Shakespeare, playwright

Courage is doing what you're afraid to do. There can be no courage unless you're scared."

—Eddie Rickenbacker, World War I hero

Hip, hip, hooray!

SIGNING YOUR FRANCHISE AGREEMENT. Finding the ideal location. Serving your first customer. When you choose to become a franchise owner, you'll have plenty to celebrate.

Here are some guidelines:

- Write celebration into your business plan.
- Match the size of the celebration to the size of your accomplishment (a glass of wine for talking to your banker, a glitzy party for your first day of business).
- Create a celebration box. Stockpile small treats and dip in whenever you achieve a milestone.
- Invite others to celebrate with you. Good cheer is highly contagious!
- Celebrate NOW. There's no time like the present to pat yourself on the back.

TIP: A steady stream of small accomplishments can make you feel more fulfilled than one or two major successes. As you dive into your franchise search, be sure to state your goals and celebrate when you achieve each one.

Happy trails

CHUCK KARPINSKE SPENT YEARS as an executive for fast-paced start-up companies, including a stint as CFO of SimonDelivers, an online grocery store, where he helped raise tens of millions of dollars in venture capital.

But while Chuck and his wife Carla enjoyed their lives, they longed to live closer to their grandchildren in Iowa. After weighing their options, they decided to make the move and pursue another new adventure: business ownership.

The Karpinskes wanted a business with recurring revenue that could take them into retirement. They also wanted to maintain their lifestyle and enjoy a flexible schedule.

The solution was closer than they realized. In fact, it was in their closets and drawers! In 2004, the enterprising couple purchased the Des Moines, Iowa, area Martinizing Dry Cleaning territory.

"Chuck and Carla have such enthusiasm for the business, and with their phenomenal sales, they have become the poster children for our franchise system," says Frank Knowles, Martinizing's director of franchise development.

Words of wisdom

MOST FRANCHISE OWNERS HAVE learned at least a few things the hard way. Use what they've learned to jumpstart your success:

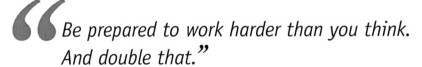

Be prepared to work harder than you think. And double that."

—Rick Toboz, Maaco franchisee

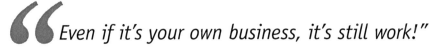

Even if it's your own business, it's still work!"

—Tony Capuano, The Entrepreneur's Source franchisee

Have a release. For me, a monthly massage works wonders for the mind, body and spirit."

—Gary Russell, Signs By Tomorrow franchisee

CAROLYN HERFURTH has helped more than 600 people make thoughtful choices about franchising and business ownership since establishing the Minneapolis office of The Entrepreneur's Source in 2002. In addition to advising clients, Carolyn writes a monthly e-letter that features client success stories and also speaks extensively on the topic of entrepreneurship and franchising.

The Entrepreneur's Source is an international franchise consulting organization that helps goal getters find and start franchises. We do this by guiding you through our focused Discovery Process, which allows you to:

- **Clarify your goals.** Through a series of interviews, questionnaires and assessments, we help you articulate and crystallize your goals along with a host of other essential criteria. Once that baseline is established, we devise a custom strategy for your franchise search.

- **Explore franchises.** Based on your goals, we recommend specific franchises to investigate. As your advocate (we are not brokers), we actively engage with you throughout your franchise search to help you determine which, if any, franchise is right for you.

Carolyn can be contacted at carolyn@e-sourcecoach.com, www.theEsource.com/CHerfurth or 952-920-0084.

BEV BACHEL is the owner of Idea Girls, a marketing and employee communications agency. Whether it's developing employee training programs, recruiting and retaining employees, motivating a sales force or promoting new products, Idea Girls delivers creative and affordable results for an impressive list of clients, including Apogee, Caribou Coffee, Ceridian, Lexinet, MarketingSalsa, Schreiber Foods and Thrivent Financial for Lutherans.

Our services include:

- **Communication.** We develop strategy, write copy, design promotional materials, create Web sites and produce videos.

- **Ideation.** We name companies, products and programs, and facilitate brainstorming sessions.

- **Training.** We develop and deliver workshops, seminars and online training programs.

Bev is author of *What Do You Really Want? How to Set a Goal and Go For It,* which has sold more than 25,000 copies and been translated into five languages.

Bev is also a frequent speaker on a variety of topics, including goal setting, creativity, writing and entrepreneurship.

For more information or to hire Bev or Idea Girls, visit www.ideagirls.com, e-mail bev.bachel@ideagirls.com or call 612-379-7166.

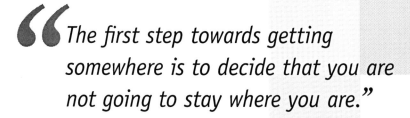

"*The first step towards getting somewhere is to decide that you are not going to stay where you are.***"**

—J. Pierpont Morgan, American financier